BAROQUE

Holly Myers

then/and

© Holly Myers, 2024.
then/and publications
ISBN: 978-1-947322-13-4

Library of Congress: 2023937527

On Nature Writing
(Or, Four Days with Others
in a Remote Place) — 5

Doctrine of
the Affections — 15

Baroque — 57

On Nature Writing

(Or, Four Days with Others in a Remote Place)

The birds go crazy even before the light. The first faint taste in the darkness of some shift in the air from this to that triggers ecstatic frenzy out there. The long day is an eternity, beginning at the beginning of eternity.

Awake-ness, here it is. (How strange that this should be age, these charged dawns. Colorless thoughts. Witness to nothing in particular, to the realness of nothing, till the birds come along. And that the young with their bright thoughts should be draped through the morning in thick sleep.) Sun.

In the valley with the creek, with the grasses, with the curtain-line of trees behind, there is a holistic bloom, a flare of joy-life-green, though the trees be of every age, grasses, shrubs, stones. The sunlight is liquid and golden. Every morning a wholly new kind of joy. Only we have memories, like spots of lichen or disease.

Why do the birds calm down when the sun is up? Are they merely shaking out their sleeping mats at 4:45? The sun brings the calmer business of the day, though even the creek, so narrow, is a booming riot.

~ ~ ~

Boulders. That's all. Granite thrusting upward as if in motion, churning through soil to make itself felt, but with a motion imperceptible to our flitting vision. (Perhaps we seem so ourselves to hummingbirds?)

Wind through grass below, a rippling sea; it is clearly what grass is made for, wind. Then up the hill from the level of the curtain-line of trees. At the peak, a pine tree was dancing as if actually to music, every branch rocking and rolling. I almost didn't see it, so far was this kind of motion from stately pine behavior. I was wrong, apparently, about that behavior, though from here, across the meadow, they stand still and tall.

Boulders—that's all. There's almost nothing to be said of boulders. To write a narrative of boulders would take millions of years. There is one, but it wouldn't even make sense.

Grasses existing up to the wind. For the wind. Offering up their little seeds.

Is nature writing even possible? The words roll right off.

Then, nearer at hand: The ant up the tree. The spider up the tree. Oh to be transported for even just an instant to that particular sense of space, that precise sensation of drive. Our drives are probably no more complicated, no less obvious from an aerial view, yet we muddle them up with our language.

Fifteen people climb a small mountain. Most know nothing about one another. A few are acquaintances. Two are related, mother and daughter. Murmurs of talk like the murmur of the creek. The daughter says to an older woman whom she doesn't know that she is looking for work that "aligns her with her purpose." Her vocabulary is stiff, like new clothes. Does it help to be insightful at twenty-three? I don't know what the mother says—she is behind, out of earshot—though she is lanky and smiley just like her daughter, in just the same proportions.

The pretty one, up ahead—she shines like a light bulb, like a flower, but flatter than a flower, less brilliant than a light bulb. There is something to her, I suppose, because she speaks very well, with knowledge and clarity, but she looks past you when she talks to her own reflection. She can't stop doing it, and probably doesn't even know that she is. She leans in as if in earnest, yet something about the contact unnerves her. There's no silence in her. She doesn't want to talk to you, she wants to talk to everyone at once.

~ ~ ~

The waxing and the waning of the long year, upon the pivot of late June. It is the waning I prefer, the shadow side. Not loss or the death of things, but the flaring of completion, as opposed to the flaring of beginning. Also, the quiet. The flaring of beginning is simple and bright, the flaring of completion is complex and resonant.

From the level of the grass, in early summer, near the solstice: softness, moistness, what variety!, delicacy, verticality, tangle, fluffy little seed pods, all stages of communion, community, with smells, the particular brightness of not-for-long and only-now, thinness and thickness, place-ness (as in, only here, only now, not moving), prickle, wet elbows, gentleness, more shapes than one expects.

A flare like fireworks of vivid yellow, tiny clusters of buds, little stamens, joyfully reaching.

Under the bill of the hat there is only grass. A perfect huge world. The ground takes the weight, all of it.

One tall dead tree and one short live one, side by side at the top of the hill. Partners. One craggy and decrepit, streaked black, the other full of needles and bushy, like a grandchild and a ghost.

From the level of the creek: constancy, variation without evolution, murmur, crinkle sound, slipping sound, ridges and curves, flow (obviously), slippery-slipping-slip-slip, fresh, gentle froth (not aggressive froth), voluminous, cohesive yet fleeting, always gone on yet always there, content within boundaries, curling, curving, a kind of deceptive gentleness or elective gentleness contingent on volume, cold certainly, loving of rocks, playful of sticks, brush and grasses gather round to adore.

From the level of the river stone: stillness, watching, being moved past, being smoothed, dry as well as wet, a dusting of old dirt, humble, soothed, calm, stable for the sake of motion, stable so as to give motion meaning, slow against fast, not too smart maybe, shaded by the adoring brush.

The grasses mat and sway at the edge of the creek. The muddy existence of mud, with its particular little creatures.

But how to even comprehend the motion-ness of the creek? It's so confusing to think about. It's here and gone, here and gone, here and gone, here and gone. It is almost still in its here-ness, yet almost always just past.

Just sit with the tree as it is, just sit with the stone as it is, just sit with the grass as it is. Why did I ever think I needed to understand it?

~ ~ ~

Frigid, the night. No warmth comes out of nothing. No warmth out of blankets themselves. Clothes themselves. Where is life if not in heat? There must be heat somewhere in there, even just a tiny pilot light.

There is something missing in the soil, I find, to give it the life of compost. My soil. Some people are brimming. Some people heat everything. Sleep comes somewhere in the night, apparently.

There are tangled dreams with erotic tugs. A very handsome young man tells you with sincerity that he's drawn to you, then he disappears. You're doing something to disrupt a performance of some kind. There is a man there you dated when very young. He doesn't seem to recognize you.

The grinding climate of poor sleep, breeding sour little shoots into the day. You're angry at this place, you're angry at yourself. What kind of monk would you make really? Needing your comfortable bed. But all of those shoots shrivel up with the first brush of outdoor air. One can't be angry at the dawn—take what it might, bring what it might. The birds have been up for more than an hour.

The sound of hot water pouring into cups, warmer somehow than the sound of cold. Footsteps on wood floors. Doors, doorknobs. More hot water, a bell. The ticking of an old furnace heating up.

I wouldn't mind the cold at all if I could find some heat in the soil within the cocoon. The cold outside is no trouble, exhilarating even. The cold inside is like a pit whose walls are crumbling away.

The ticking of a clock. The faithful hum of a radiator in an empty room. The faithful quiet of an empty room. A good one is better than all of us combined. But it is short-lived: footsteps. More footsteps. More hot water. Us all with our petty revelations, our sproutings and bloomings and right and wrong choices. The room was empty all night, you could have come then? A night room is different somehow. More hot water. Spoons rattling. No voices, thankfully. A few exhalations. Let them keep their good and dull selves within for a while, their generous and less generous thoughts.

Then the sun slips the bounds of the opposite hill and floods the meadow valley with gold. A whole new kind of joy, one more time. Believe like the grass (the grass says), offering up its diamond droplets to the light.

Doctrine of
the Affections

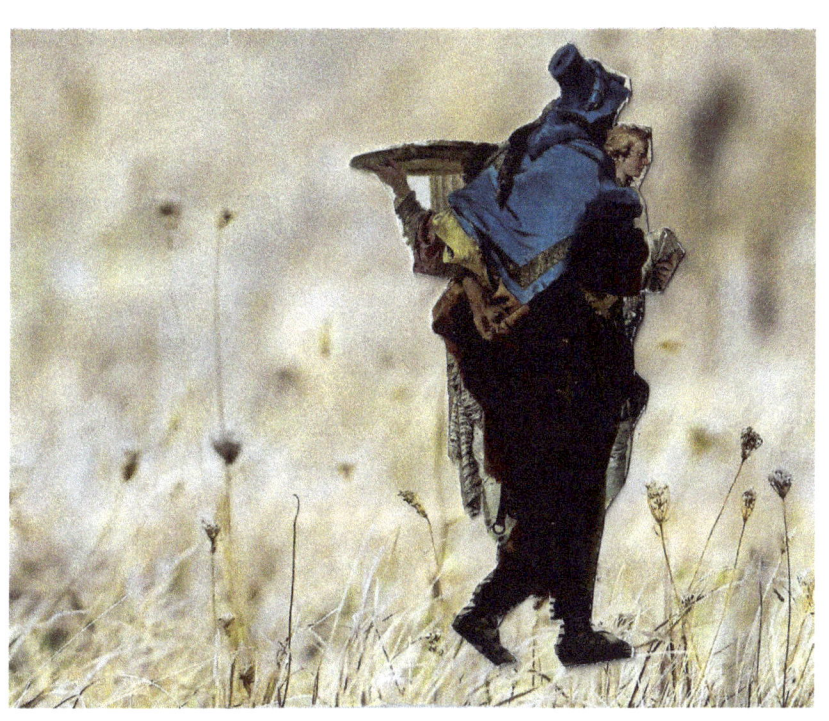

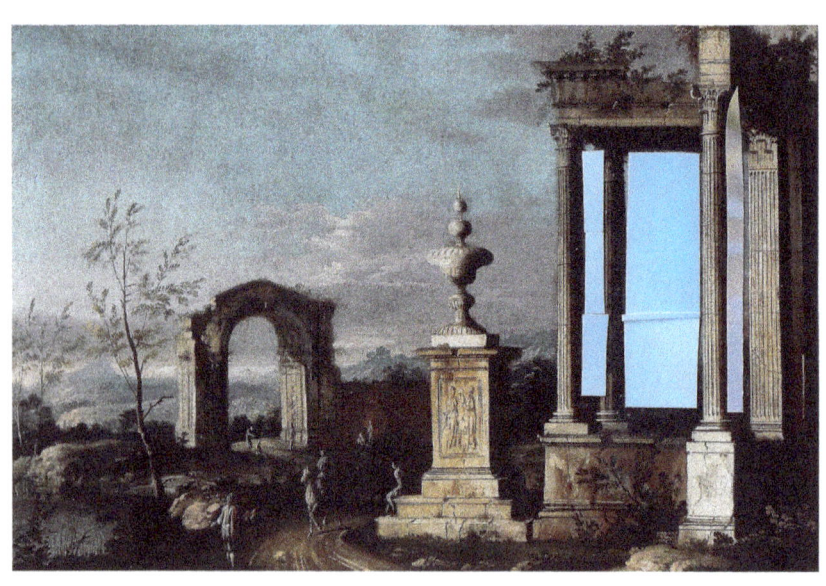

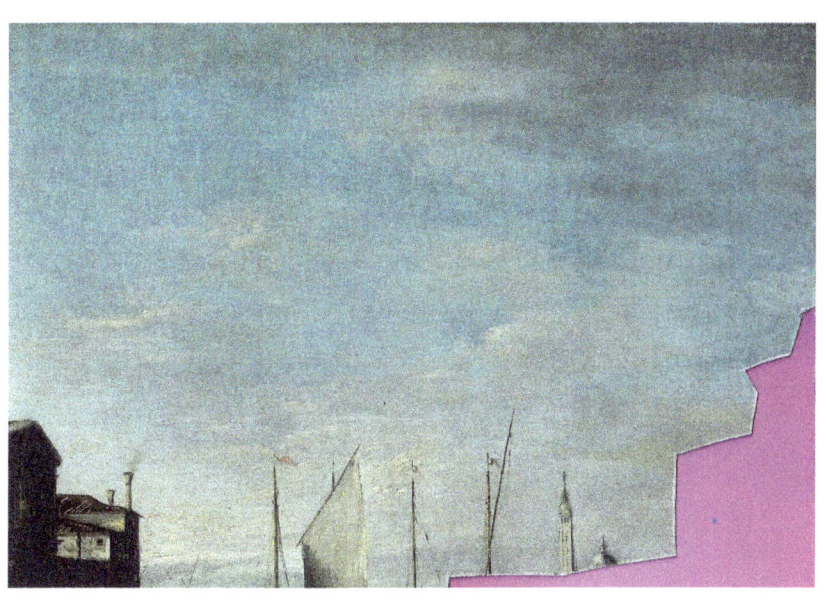

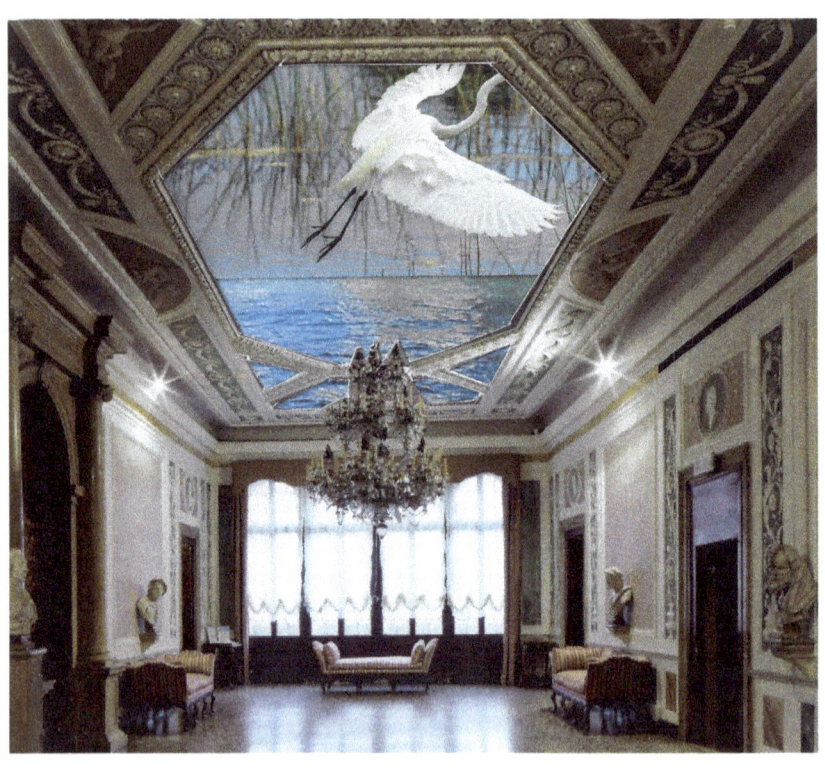

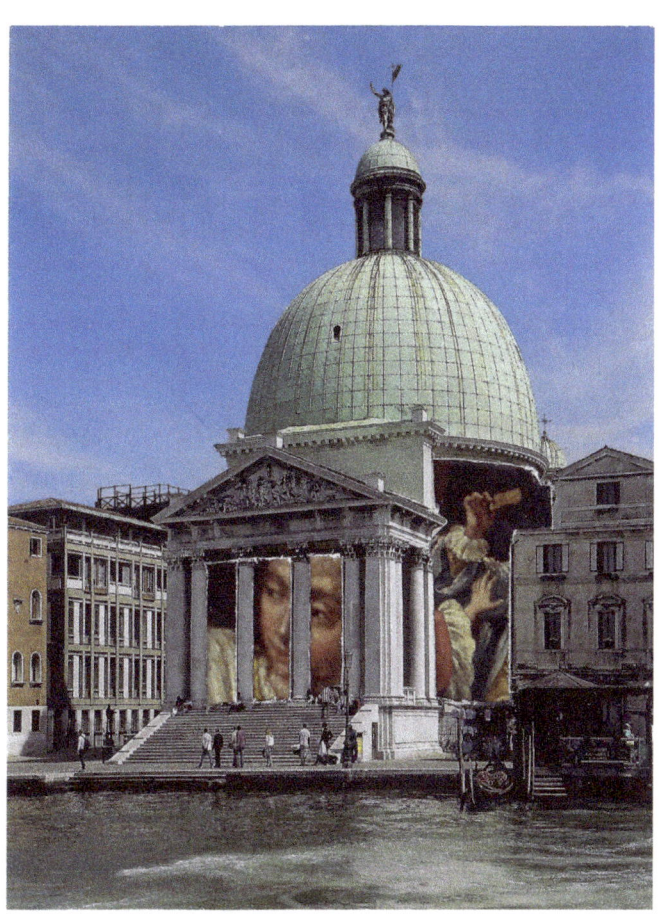

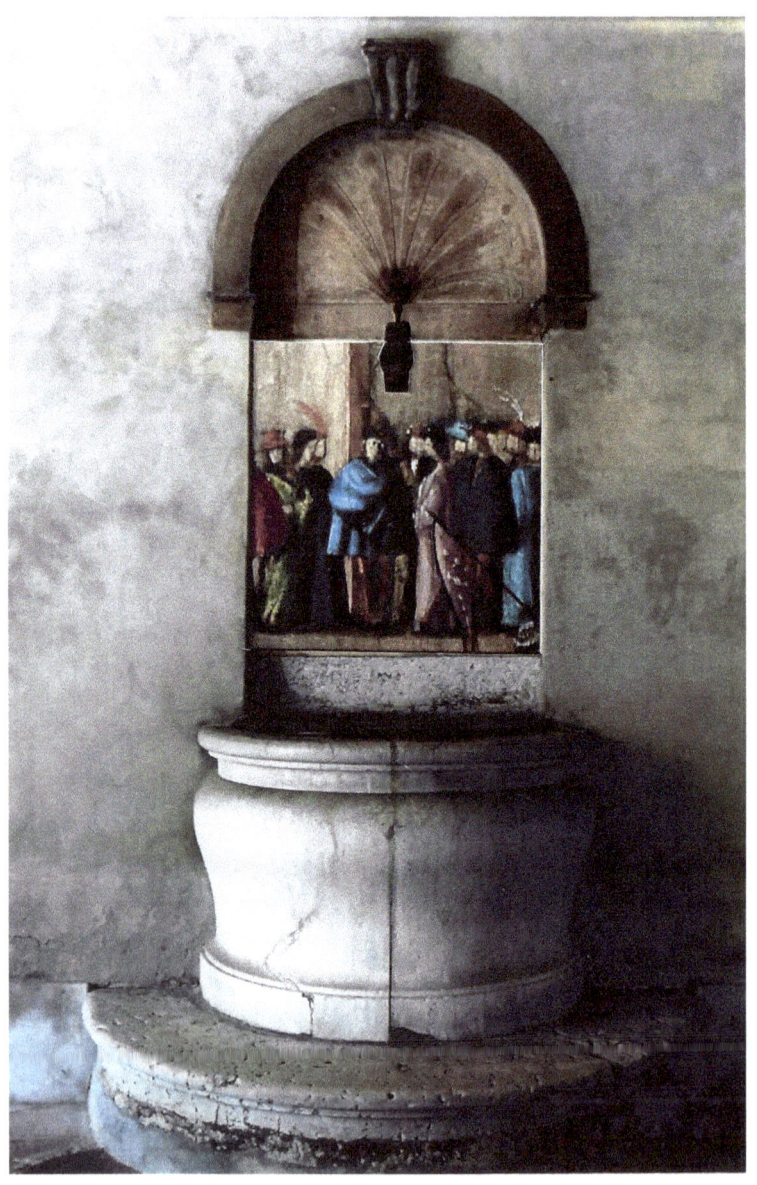

22

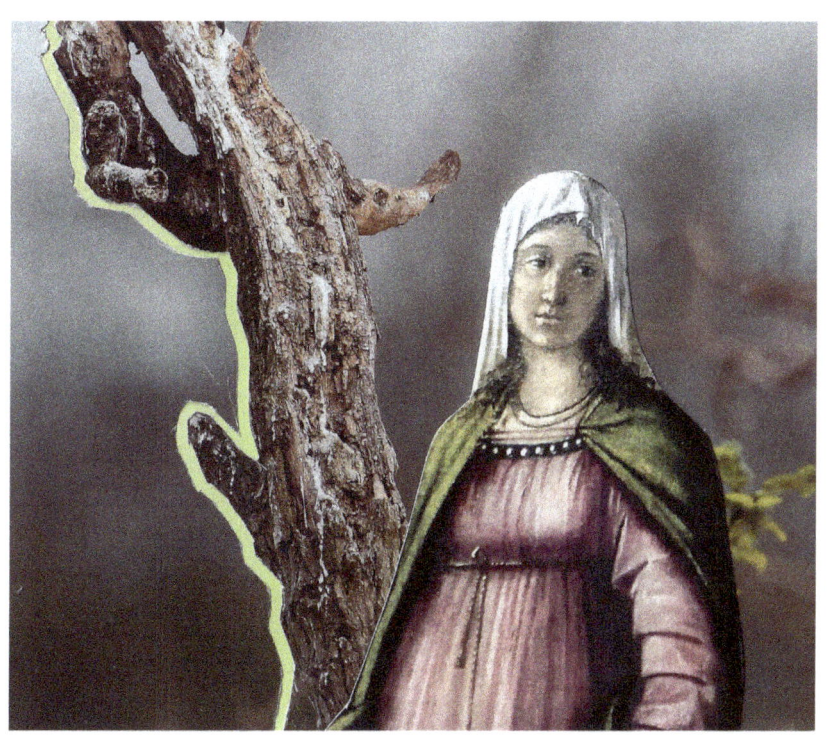

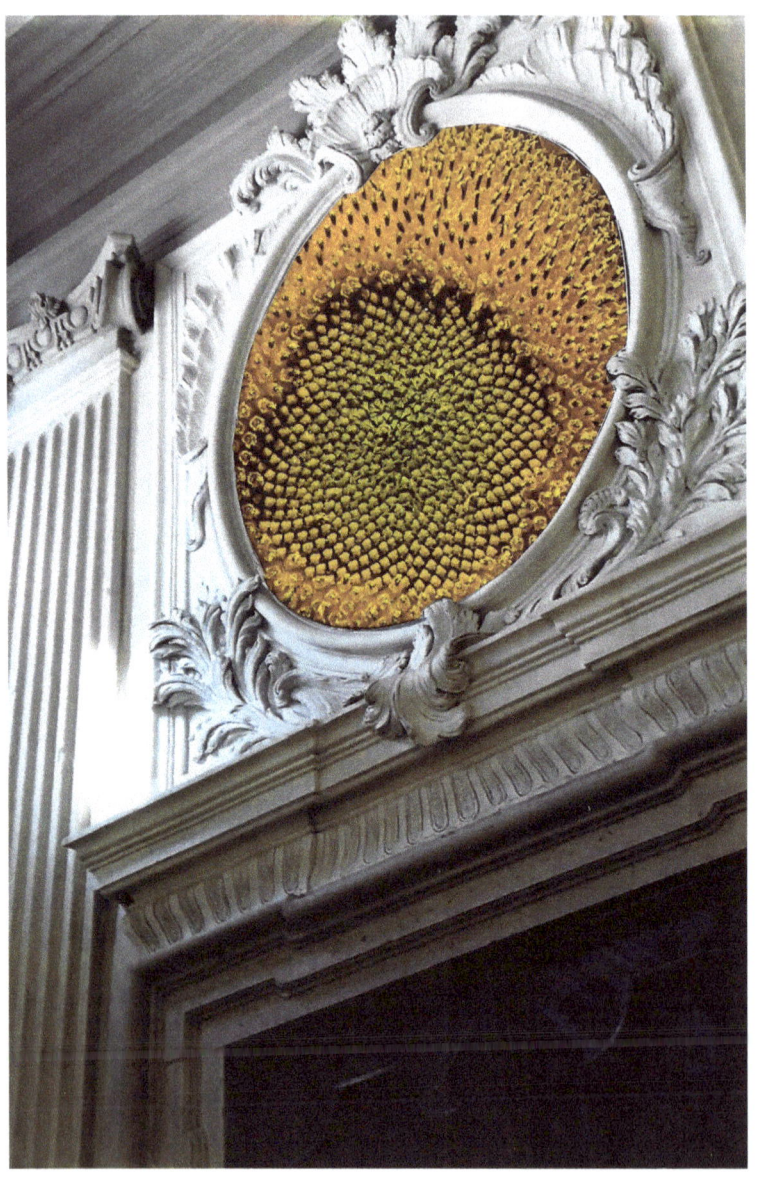

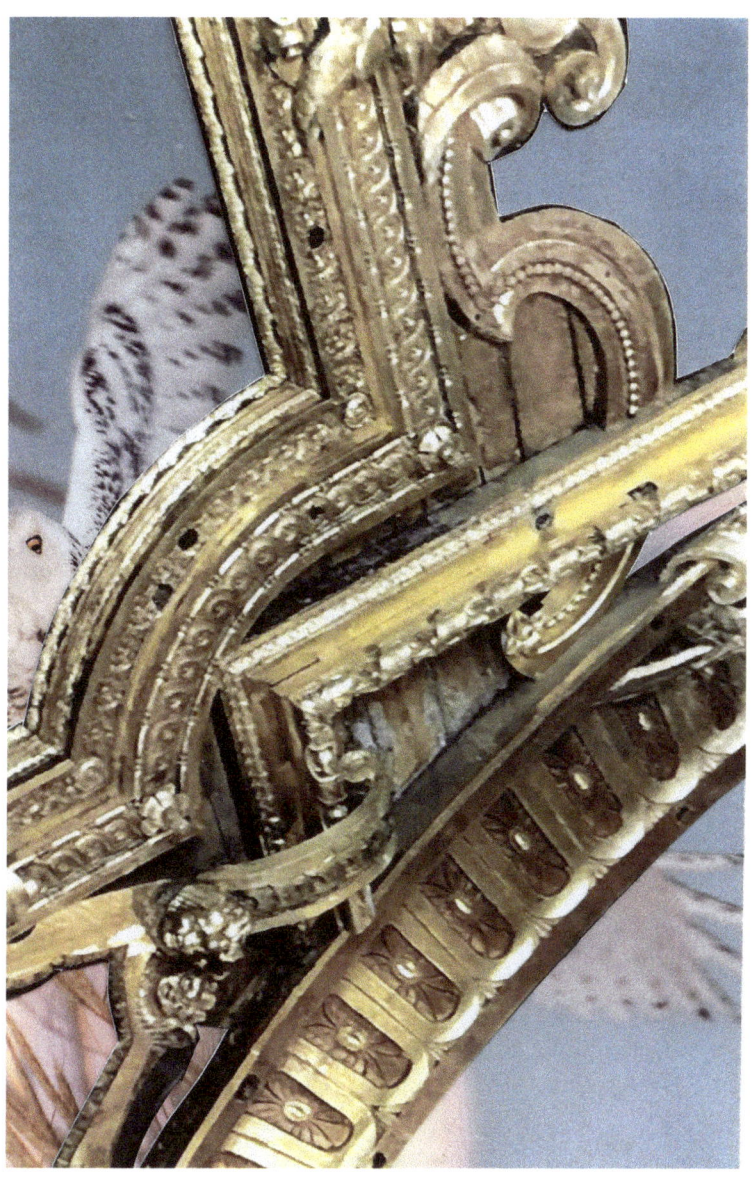

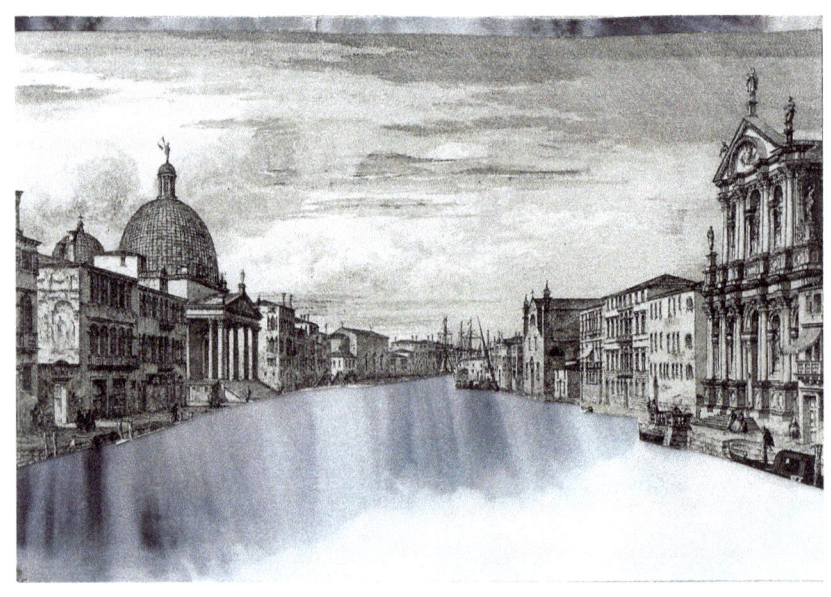

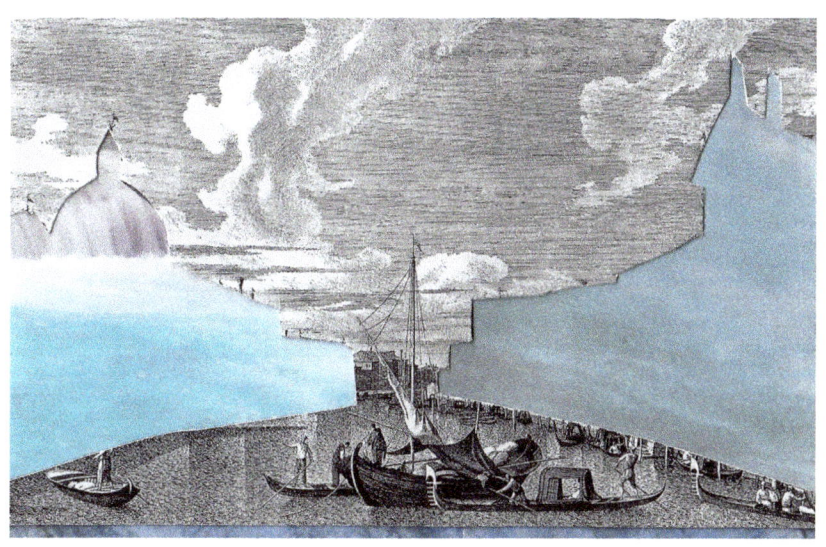

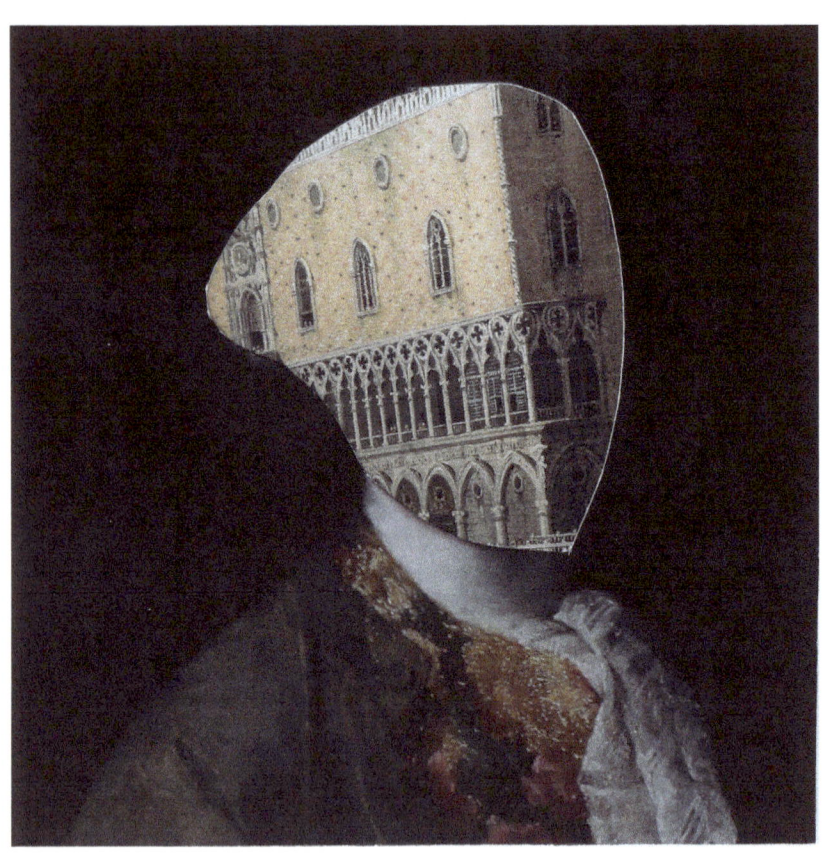

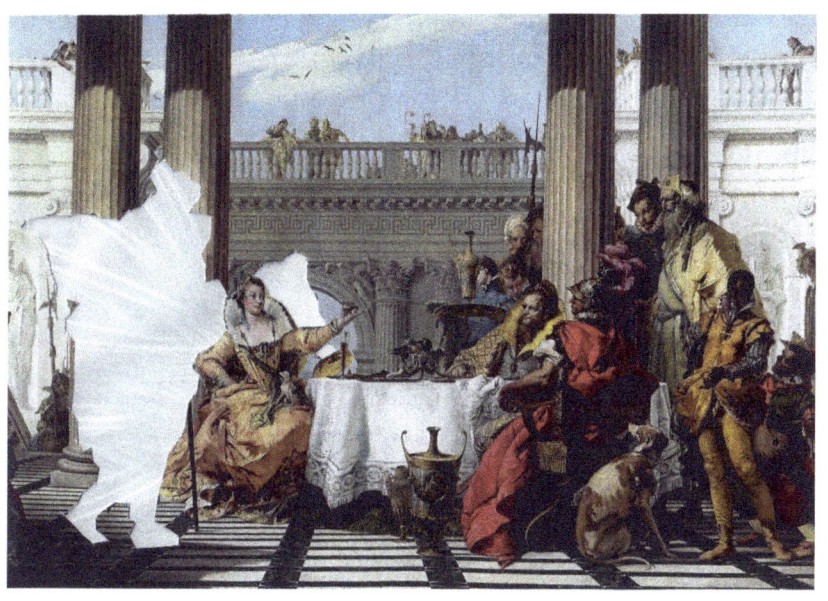

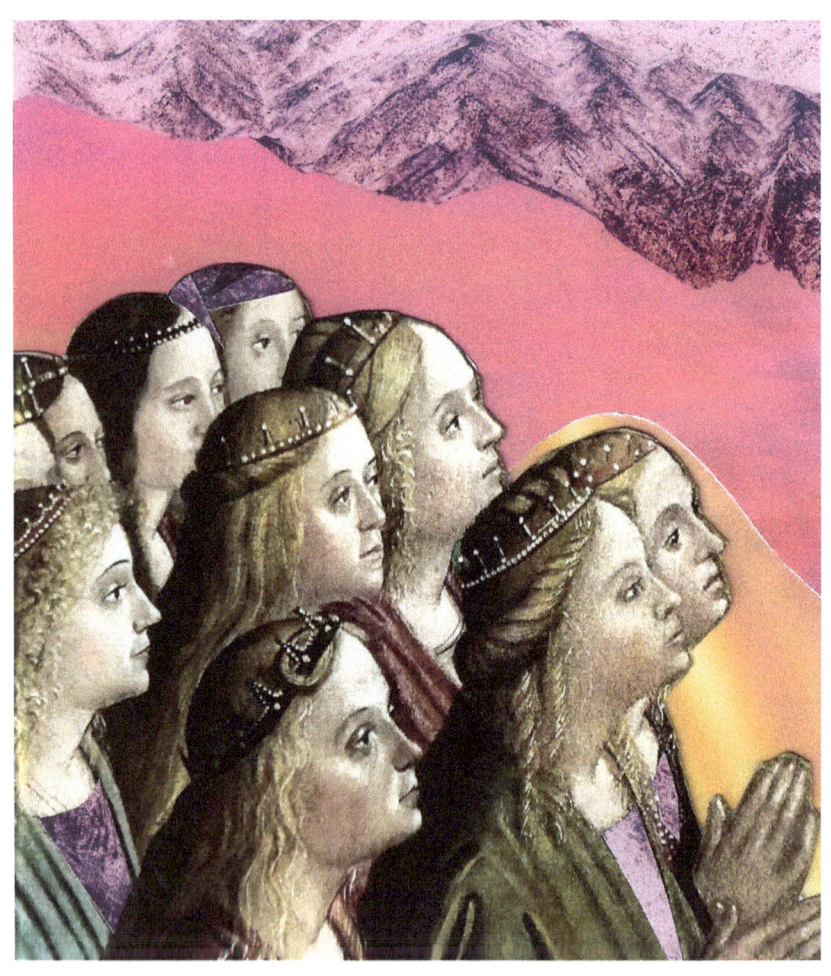

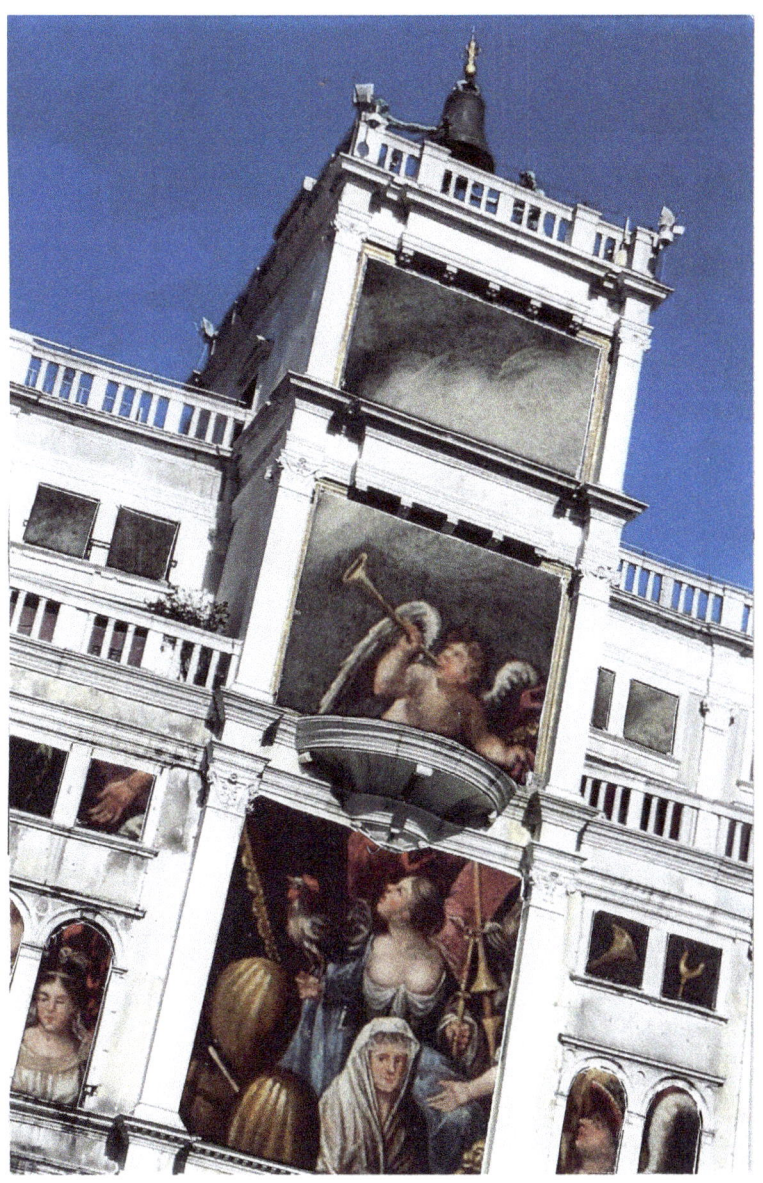

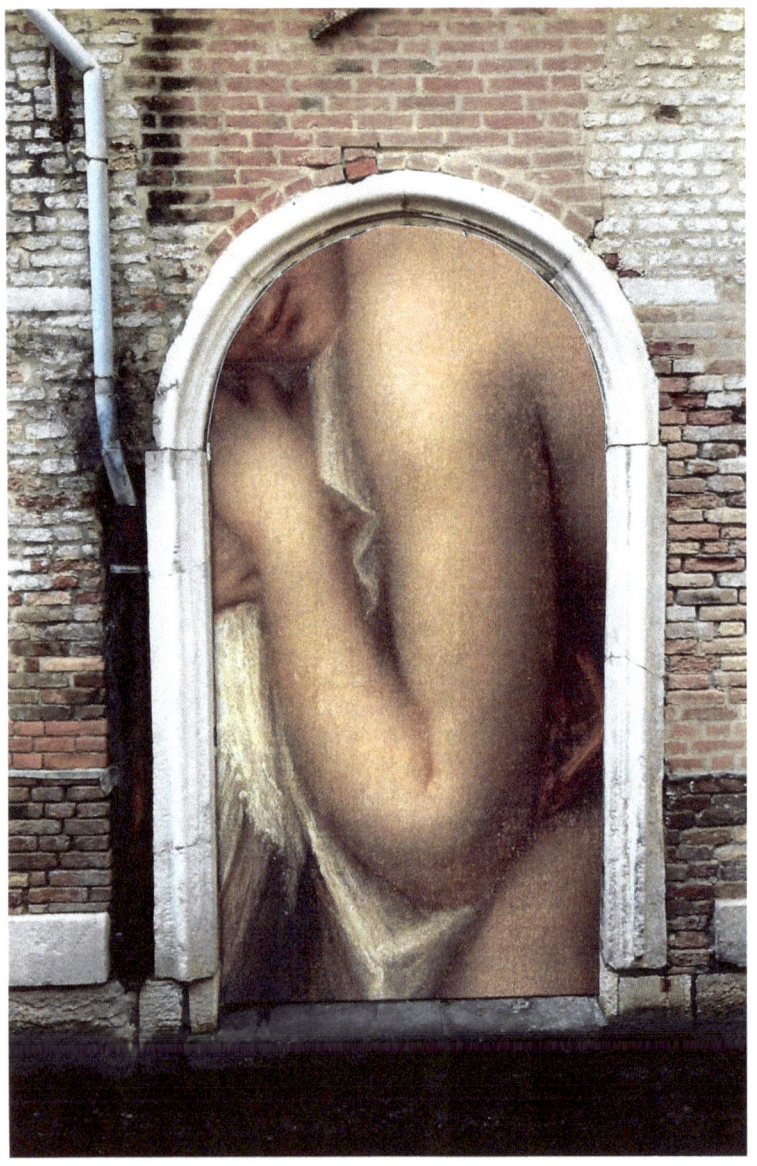

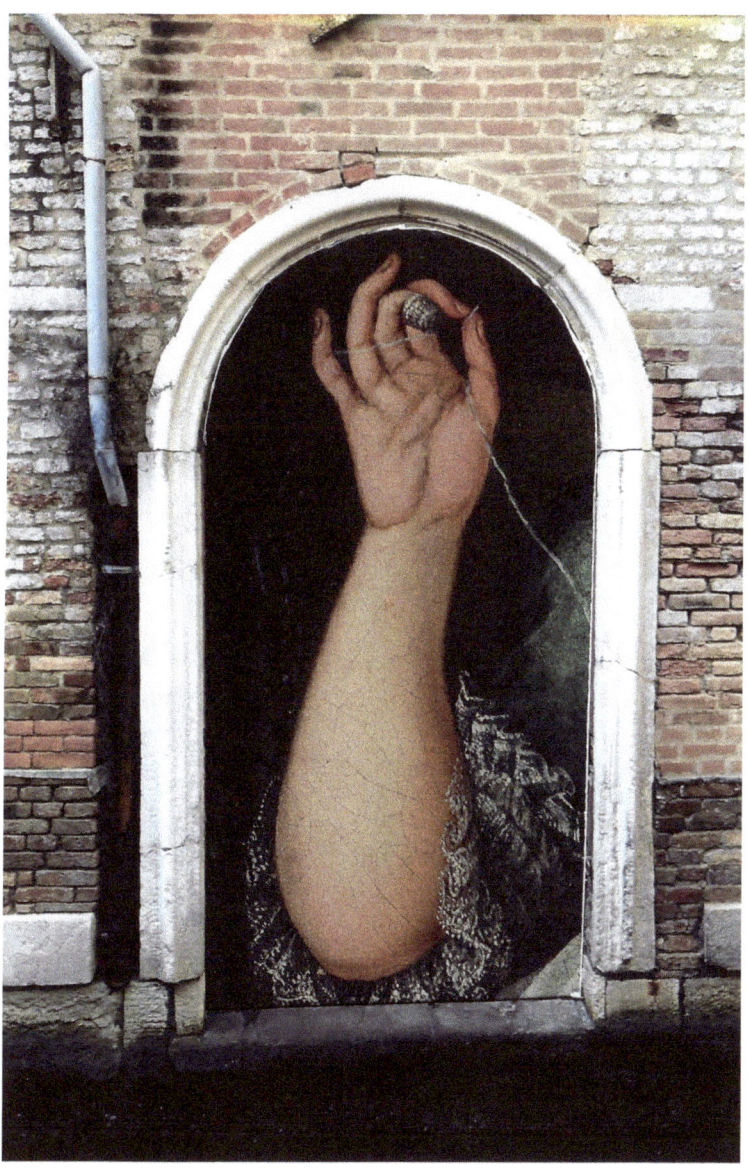

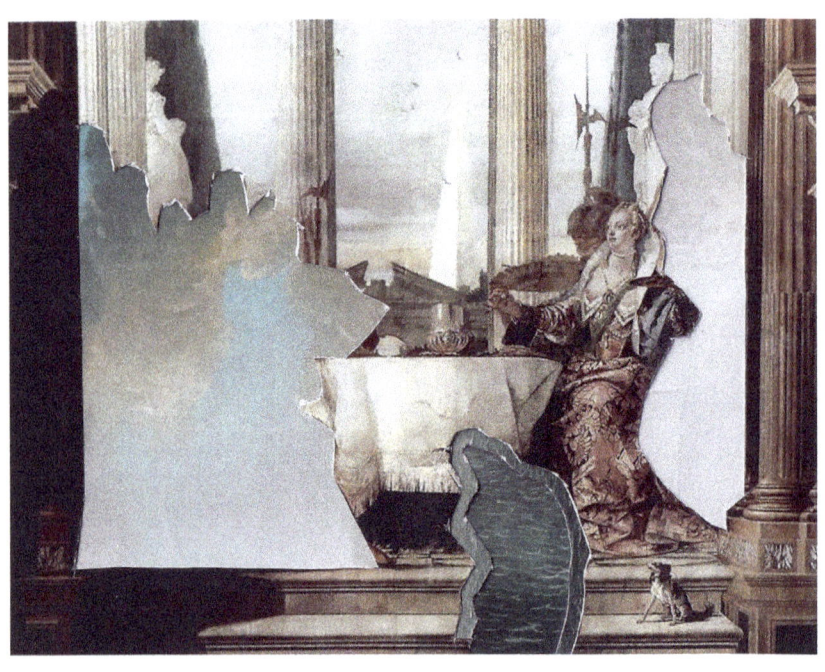

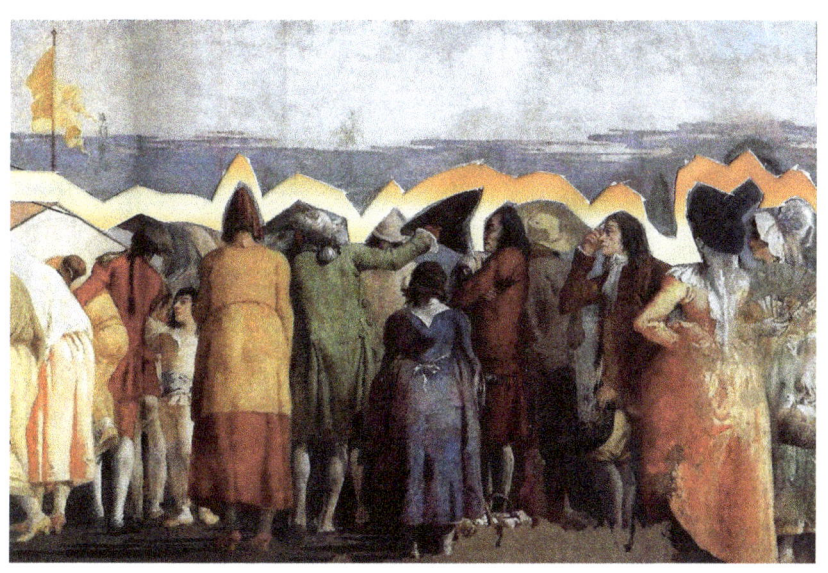

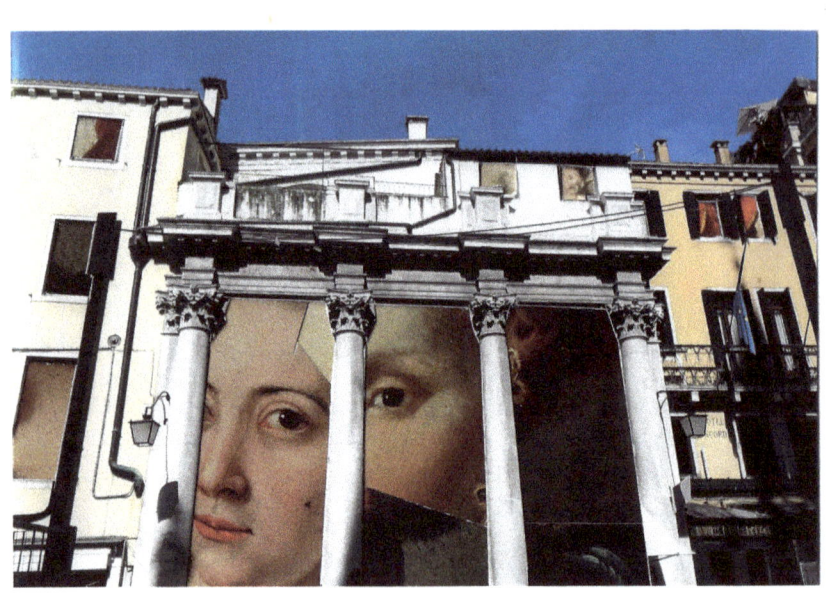

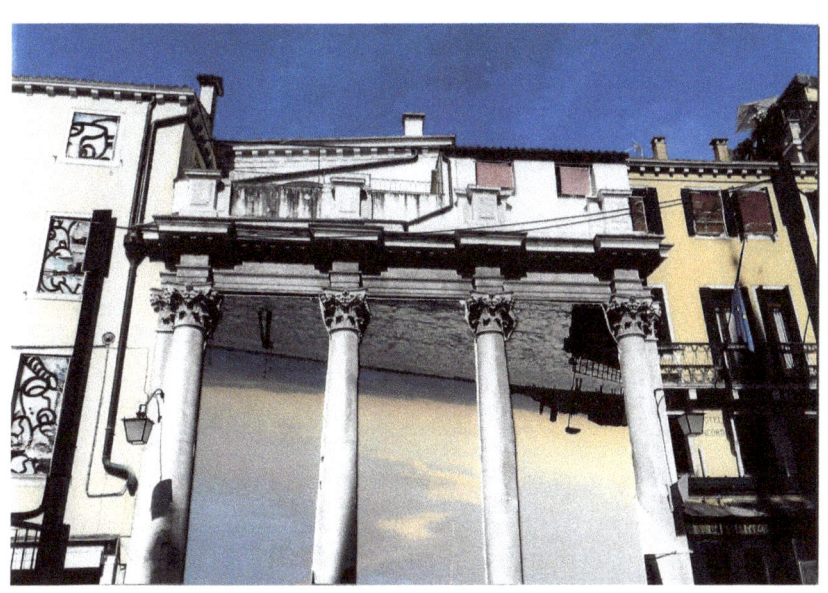

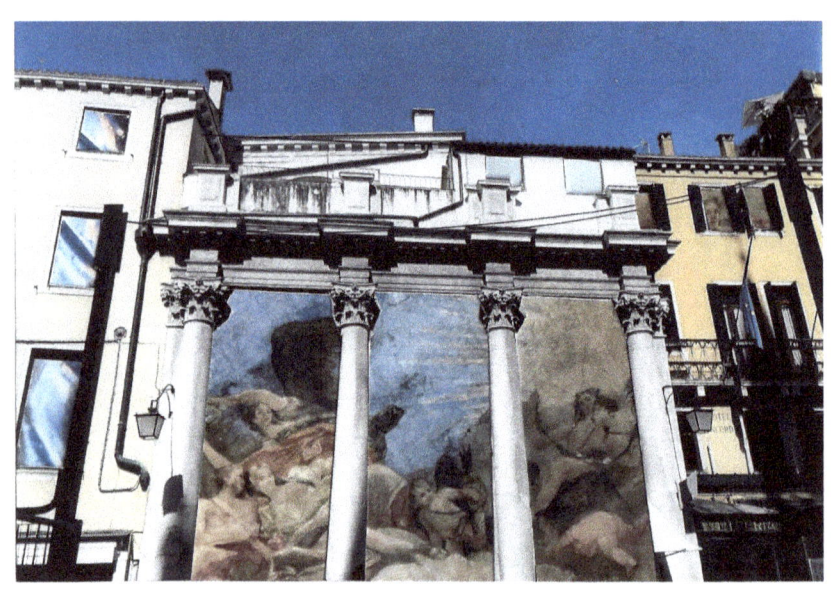

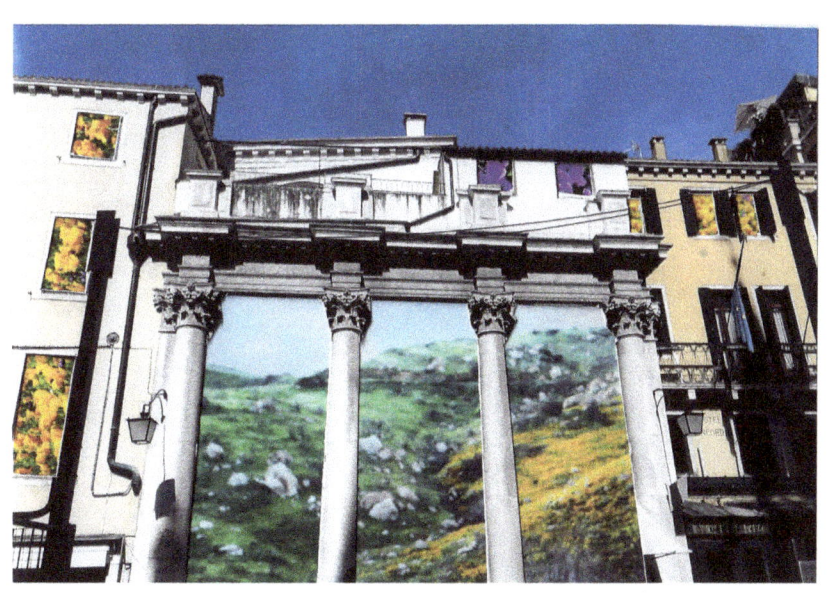

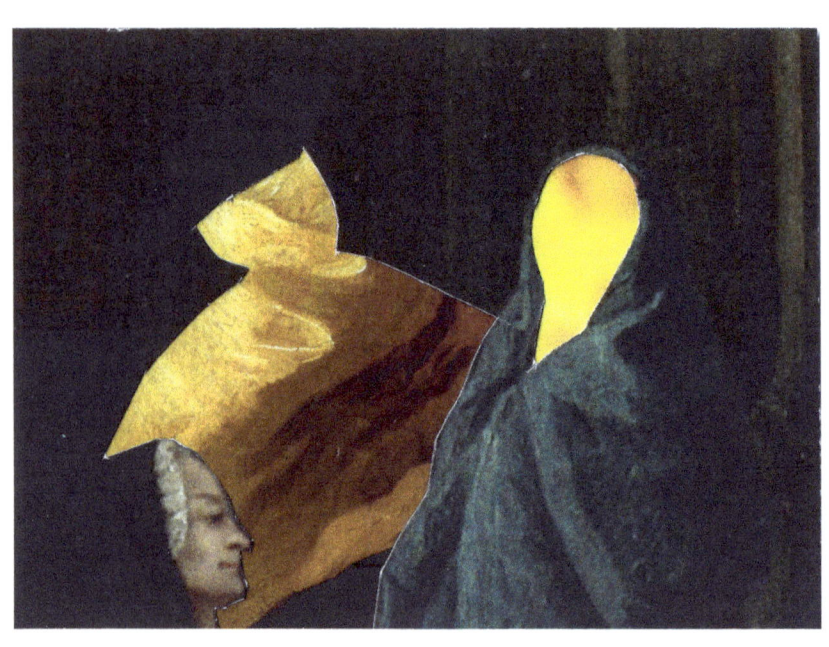

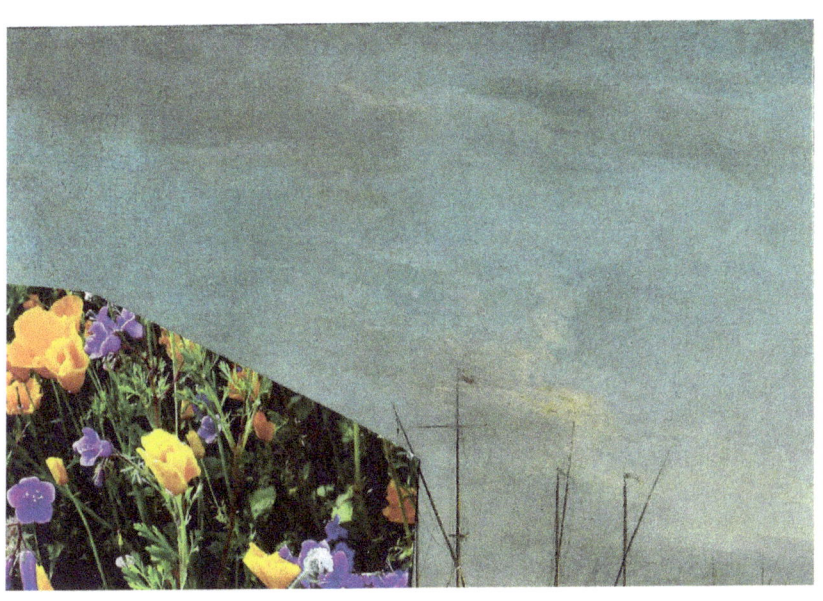

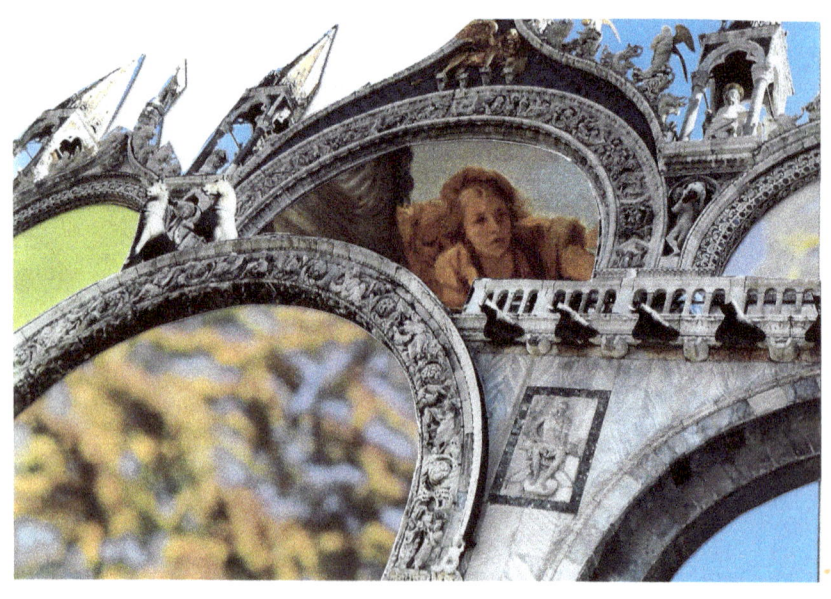

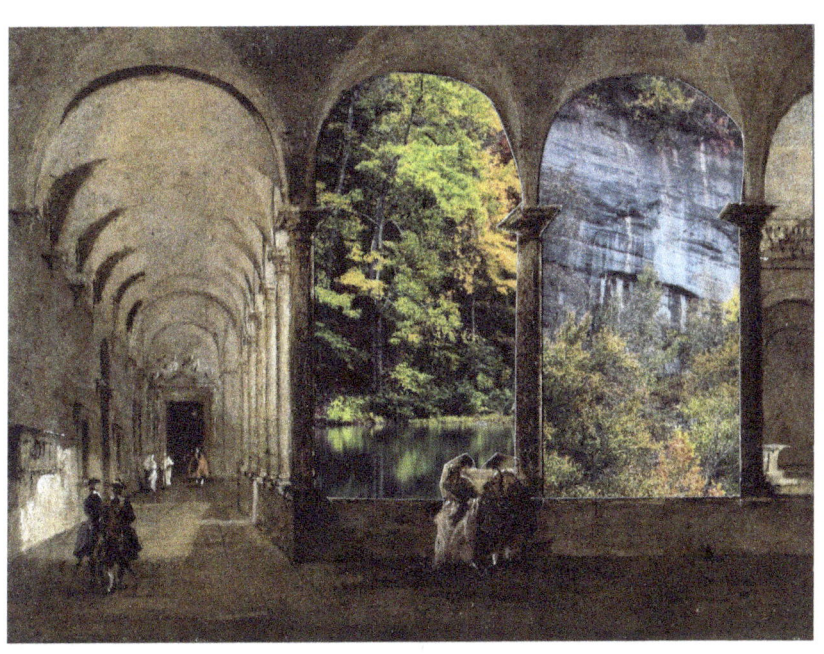

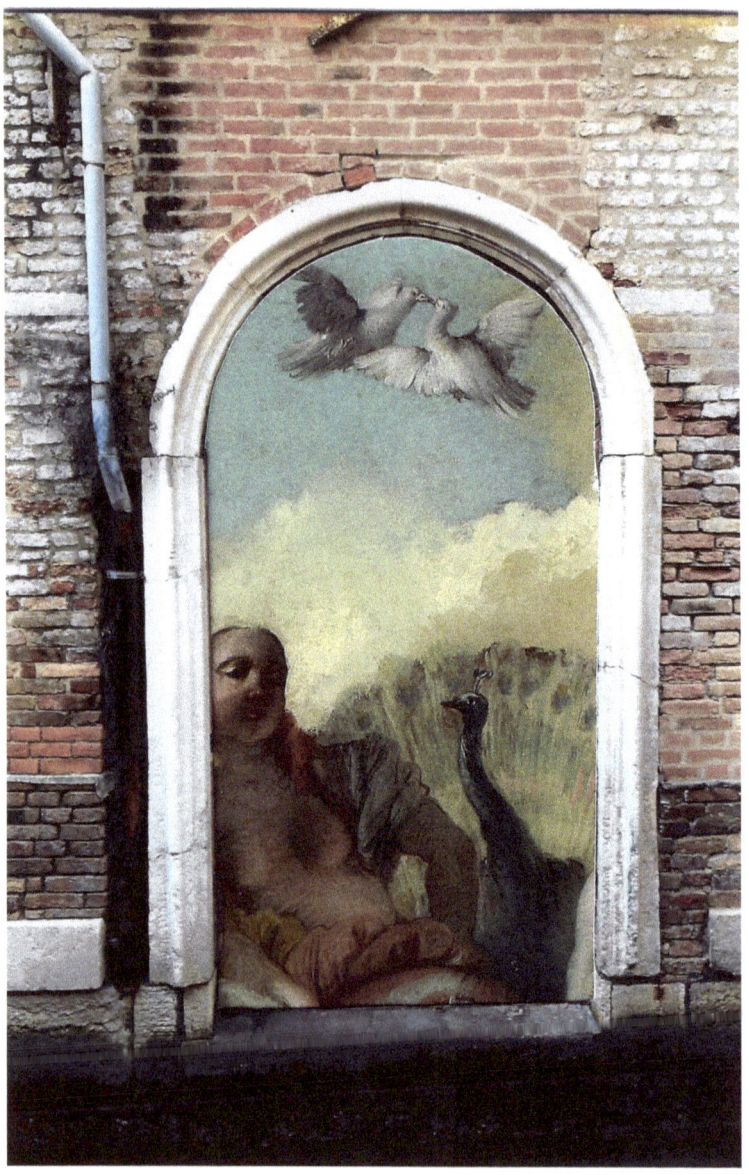

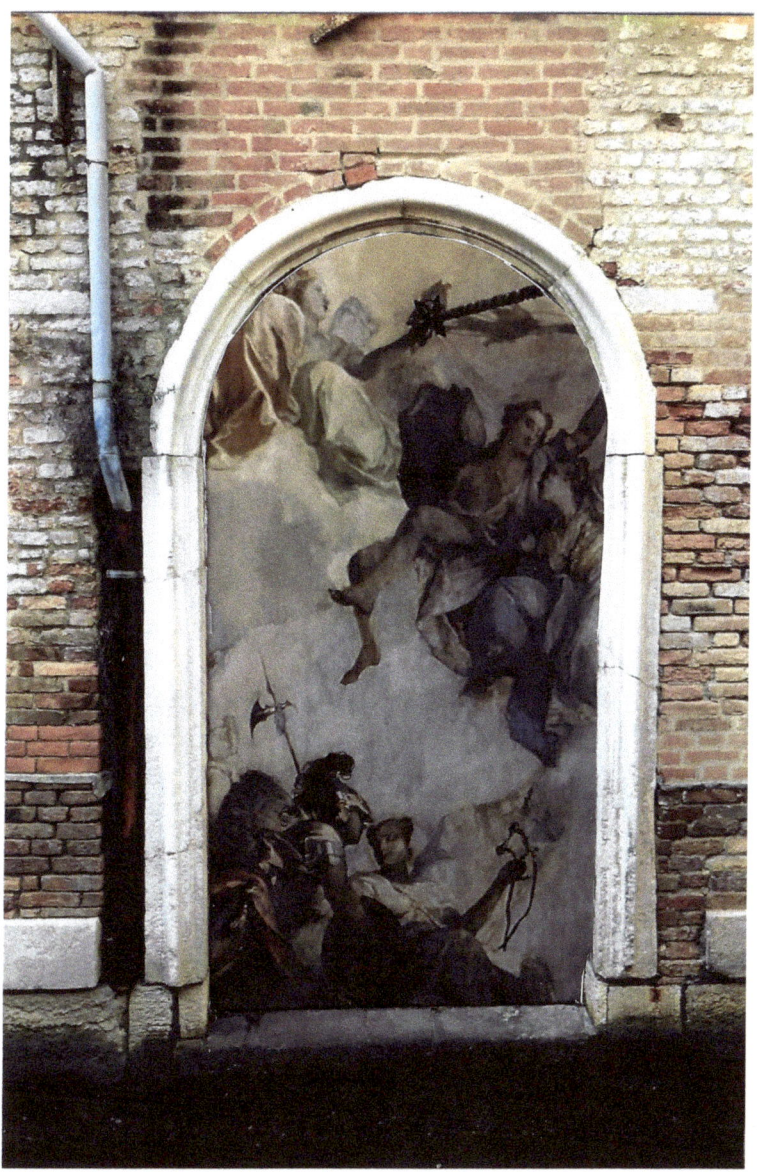

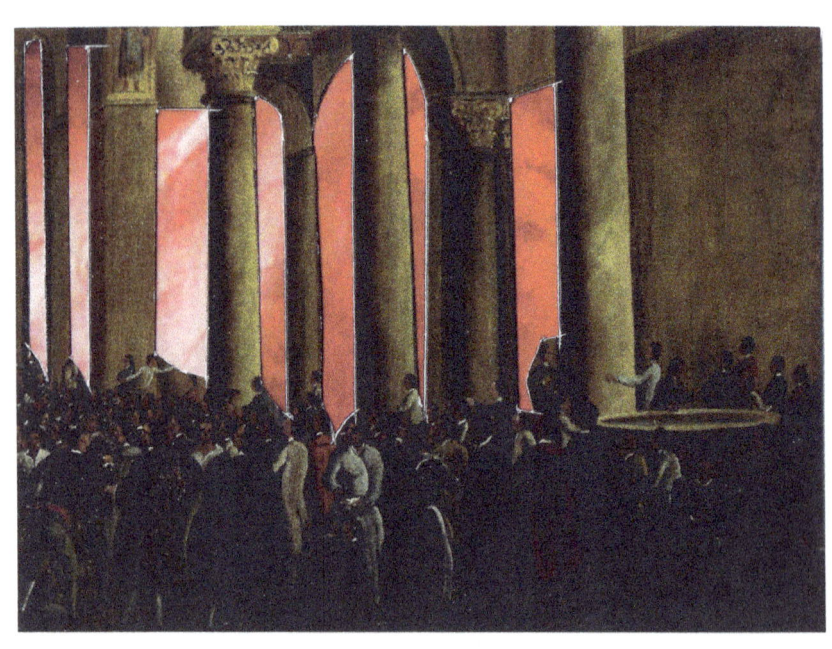

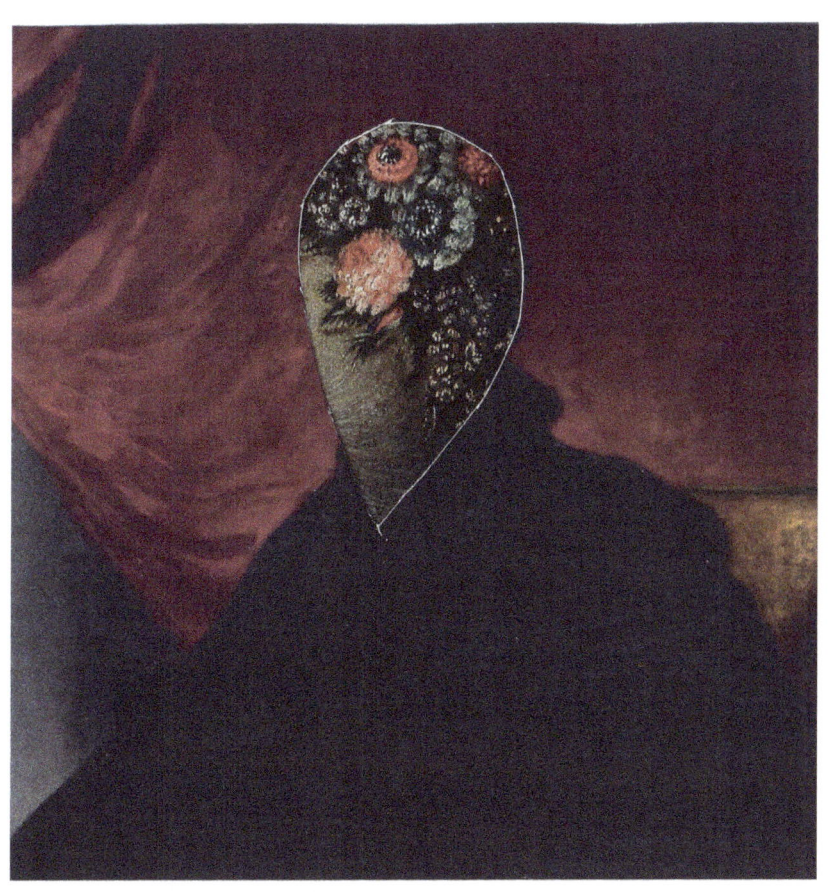

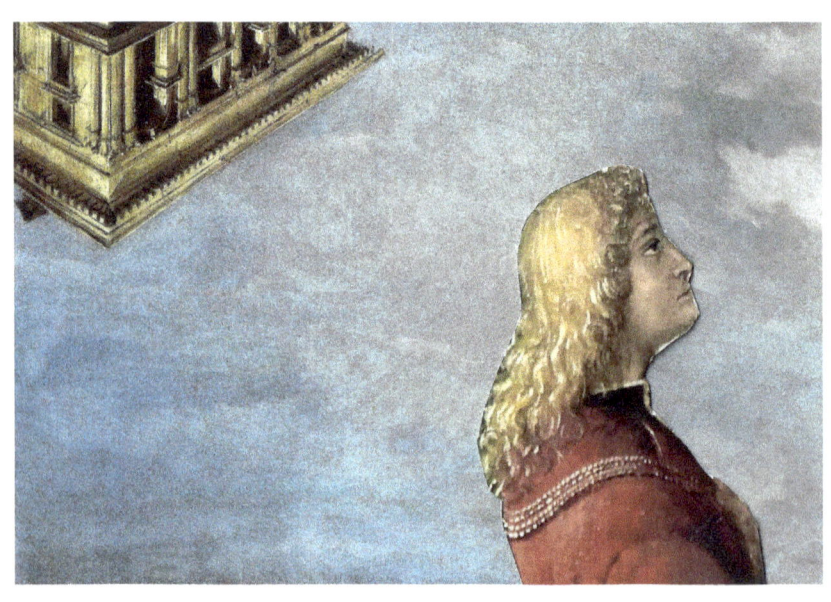

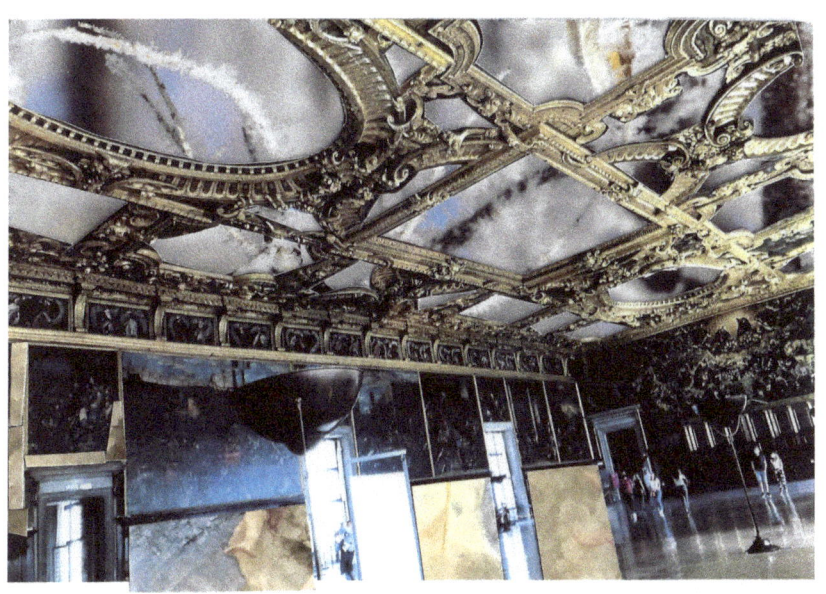

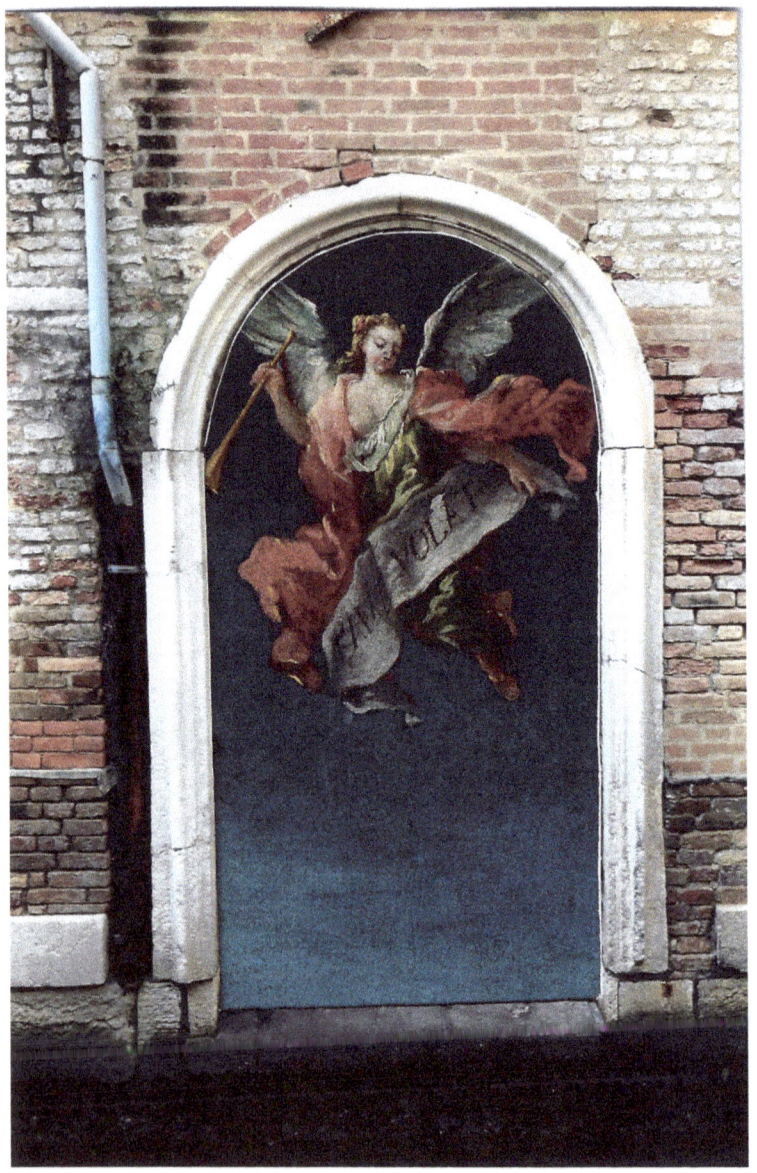

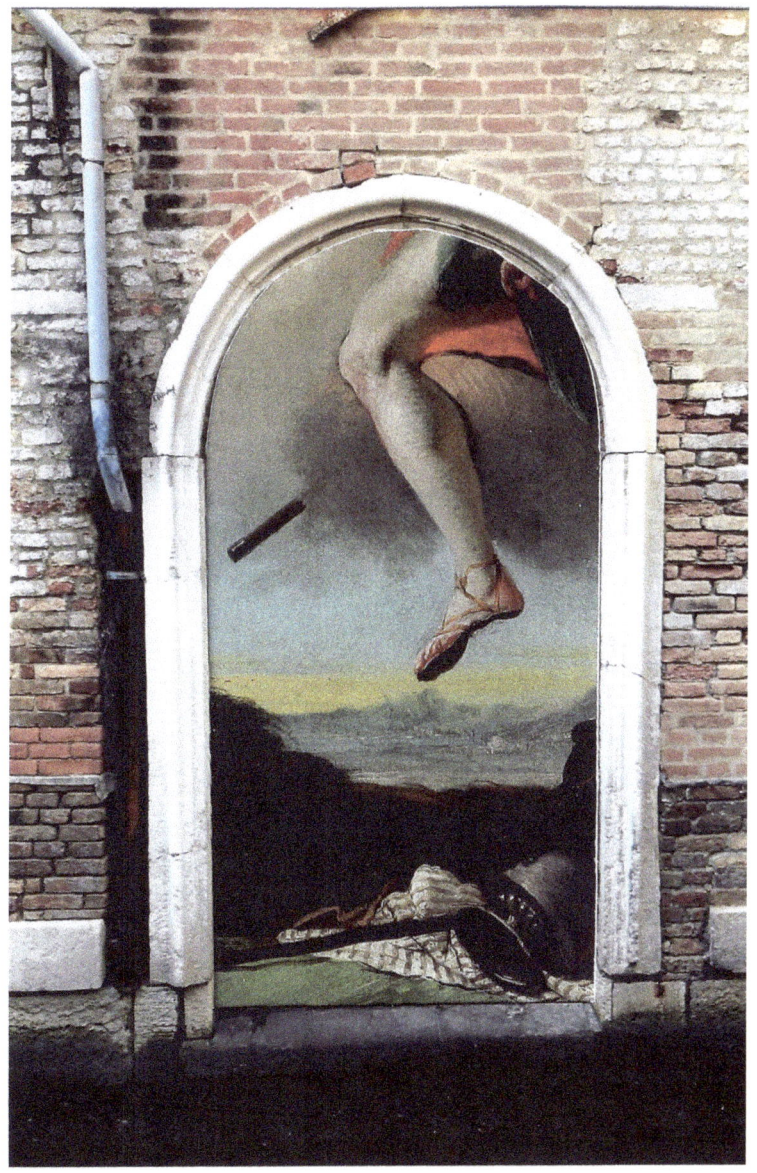

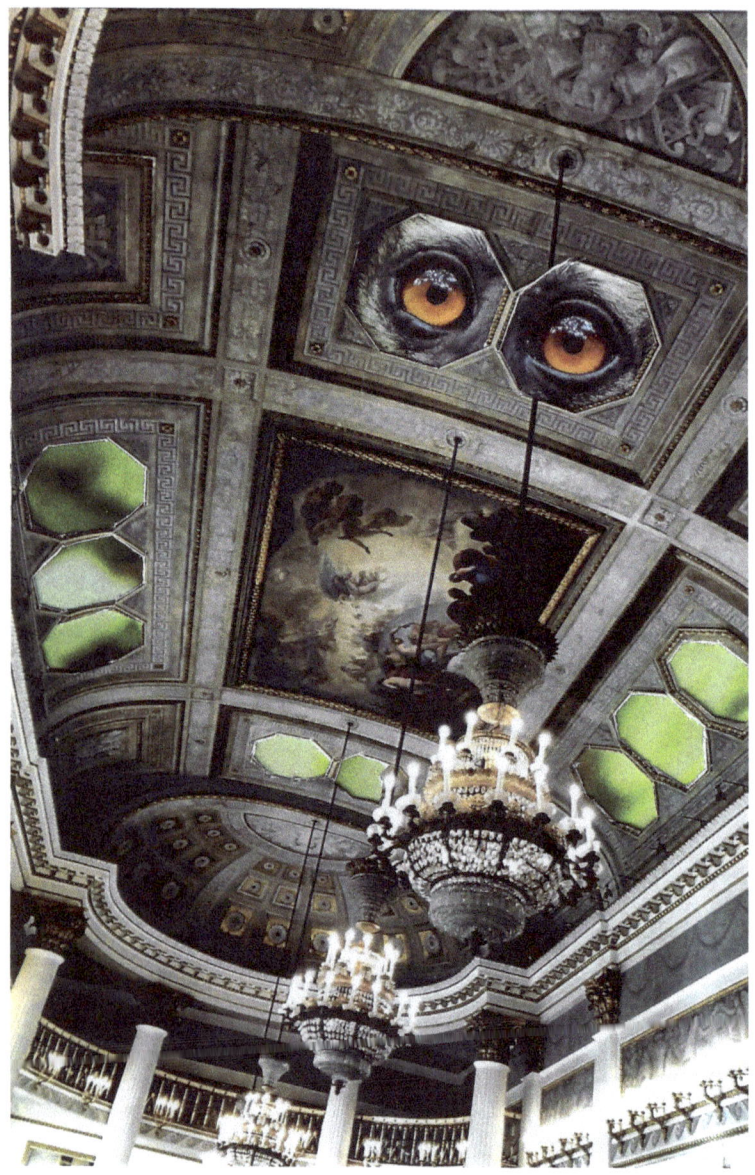

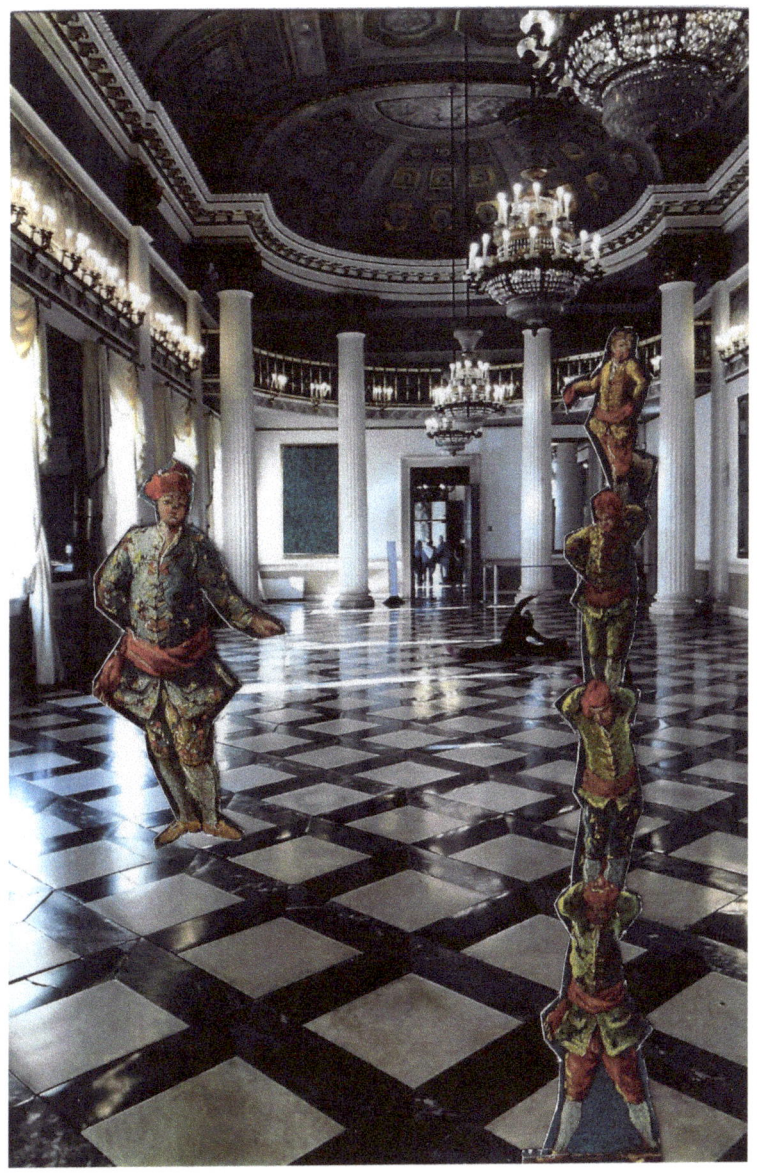

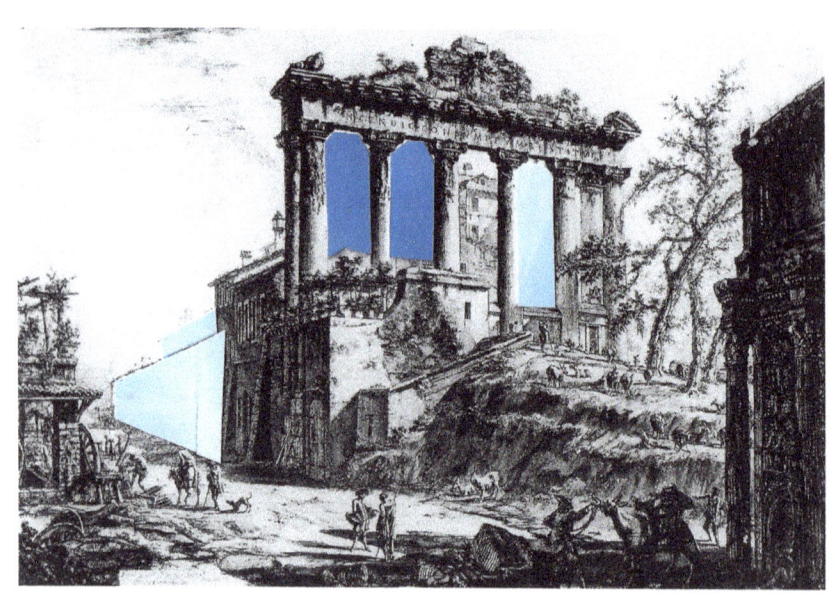

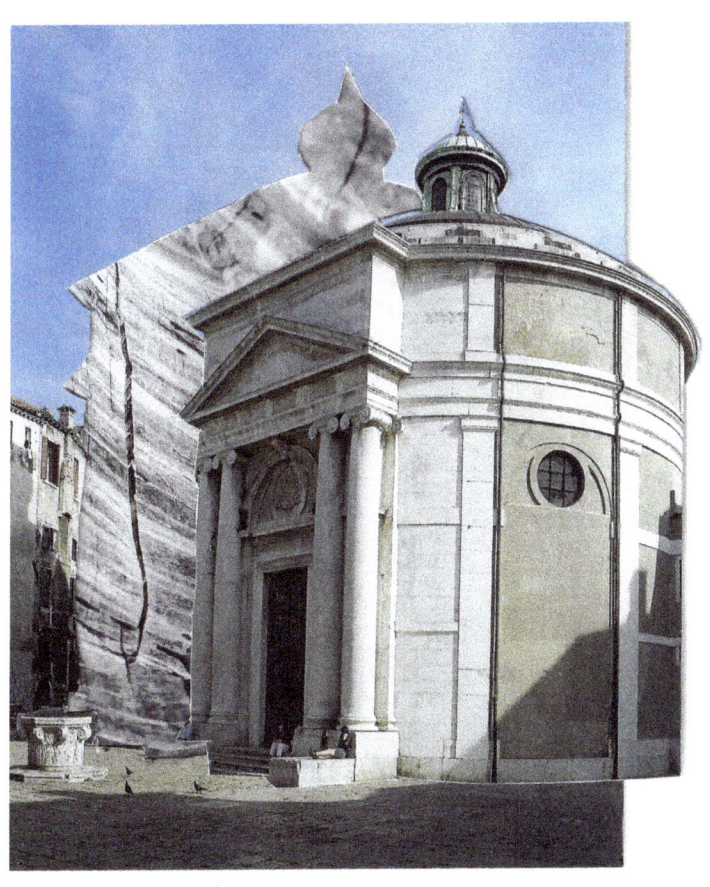

Baroque

In the restaurant, which is small, the ladies all have beautiful shoes. They laugh gaily and in comfort, in their own language, which is a beautiful language, and their shoes have a life of their own down there, as components to the sort of women they are, women who live with centuries behind them, without resisting the current of time.

You, in the corner, have traveling shoes, and that is hardly the only problem. You changed them furtively just outside the door, stuffing worse shoes out of sight somewhere, but it was not enough. Everything about you has been crumpled in a suitcase, and too large a suitcase, along with too many other things, with too little coherence between all the things, for too long. You believe yourself apart from history. Can that ever be true? You believe you were severed long before your birth, that it wasn't your fault or any choice of your own, and you can't in fact imagine it otherwise. Sometimes you see it as a kind of freedom. But what are you left with? Look how you cower.

Their shoes gleam like well behaved dogs, flashing periodically from under the table, flirting along the hem of the cloth. There is very little to them, these physical objects, just a few small patches of perfect leather, half an inch or less between the skin and the street, and a heel like the column of one's very own temple, supporting a self that is of course almost weightless. Their perfection lies in their finding within themselves, in moments like these, however fashionable, however expensive, the dignity to be altogether forgotten. The ladies are arrayed at the large, round table in the front, in the window, with their men, and at other small tables here and there among mirrors, and they all, mutually, forget their shoes, and the beautiful bags that hang from their chairs.

~ ~ ~

1. *Characterized by ornate detail. Plentiful and intricate ornamentation. Stylistically complex, even contradictory.*

Inside is a cauldron. It is nearly shapeless. There is a sloshing sound. Encroaching round the edges is a perception of containment, but where exactly? And how? Containment means walls. But where is the inside definitely not?

The inside swells to fill a small, momentarily empty piazza. Its footsteps ring upon old stones. It draws in again like an inhale through a narrow corridor, then expands into another piazza. The inside is liquid but without texture. The walls are borrowed walls, like those of a riverbed.

~ ~ ~

2. *Absurdly complex. Bizarre and uselessly complicated. Highly adorned and tormented.*

The outside of the inside is porous and charged. It has a sucking quality. It sucks at the world, draws into itself that which covers it, whether temporarily or periodically or permanently. Bare and raw at first, as if chemically unstable. Wet plaster is something almost obscene, sucking up pigment and any kind of impression. Before you know it, whole worlds unfold, dissolving the surface into atmospheric visions.

(Temporary: touch. Periodic: clothes. Permanent: tattoos and scars.)

~ ~ ~

History: The surface of the world overgrew itself and monks in sandals stormed the countryside waving their fists in disgust. And what is society but a sloshing cauldron, a system seeking equilibrium. In beauty is contained the elements of decadence, and in decadence necessarily injustice; in ornament lies a betrayal of form. Some part of the world seized and righted itself, withdrew its curling leaves and cherubim. Jesus emerged as a man among men and the chapel walls went suddenly quiet.

But as the bare wet plaster dried and glared, humanity trembled and also grew bored. Look inward, said the walls. So humanity, famished, turned upon itself and found within itself the feast of sin. There is no end to the ornament, the complexity, the excess there. For a time the surface of the world lay fallow while humanity, gorging only upon itself, grew sick. Poisoned by itself, it made war with itself, burned itself on open pyres while it cheered and chopped itself up into bloody pieces. Jesus, hitherto strident with democratic conviction, now sat moaning with his head in his hands.

Then bishops in robes with golden threads reappeared dangling sparkling objects from their fingers. Humanity, blood-smeared and dripping with sweat, looked up from the carnage, crawled out of itself toward the sparkling objects and the surface of the world quivered and moistened once more, began to sprout. Jesus departed altogether and Mary emerged in plumes of coral and indigo satin, bathed in a sphere of golden light. She tipped her beautiful head to the left and Judith severed the head of Holofernes. The bare wet plaster, revived, began to twist and strain and burst into legions of flowering vines, leaves like the open palms of hands. The satin billowed, parted, slithered down between pale white thighs and Venus rolled once more into being, reaching for Adonis. Amid the foliage, humanity was pacified. The cherubim returned with a piping sound. For in boredom, they piped, lies the elements of oblivion.

~ ~ ~

3. *Complexity, confusion, and excess.*

Angels tumble from the clouds in spirals.

~ ~ ~

4. *The desire to evoke emotional states by appealing to the senses, often in dramatic ways. Grandeur, sensuous richness, drama, vitality, movement, tension, emotional exuberance, and a tendency to blur distinctions between the various arts. Paradoxically both sensuous and spiritual. Vivid views of the infinite. A new sense both of human insignificance (particularly abetted by the Copernican displacement of the Earth from the center of the universe) and of the unsuspected complexity and infinitude of the natural world.*

In the restaurant, you sit with your back to a mirrored wall. Is this a joke?, this mirror. You are ashamed. You try not to think of the back of your head and the uncoordinated slope of your shoulders. You watch the ladies who make their mark on mirrors, for whom mirrors were actually made. They laugh gaily and enjoy their lives, flirting through their shoes. The mirrors expand the space like breathing and smudge out the boundaries where the walls had been.

When you return from the bathroom you walk up to meet yourself.

~ ~ ~

Beauty is an instable force. It gathers mysteriously even out of its absence, beginning as a transparent sheen, little more than a certain perception of moisture. Out of ugliness even. Like a mold it grows, then like a moss; suddenly it's covered in little petals. It coheres, burgeons, builds, drifts. Shapes form and pile, almost tumble, look as if to tumble, hold, tumble more; the mechanism is crystalline. It loves itself, beauty. It consists almost entirely of love of itself. It burgeons with the force of love of itself into a dozen, a hundred, a thousand petals, and the petals harden into facets, a thousand facets, facet upon facet, all glinting and flashing for one another, for the benefit of one another's praise.

It contains within itself, this burgeoning force, the elements of intoxication, innocuous at first, in small quantities, like arsenic. The intoxication has something to do with the love. Love has something to do with lust. Beauty spreads and builds, driven on by lust for itself, until it becomes even by its own vertiginous logic impossible. It trips over itself. Intoxication leads to folly, folly to frenzy, and frenzy to psychosis, which by its very nature fractures. Beauty, hard and crystalline at its root and increasingly outward from its root as it grows—it fractures. It splinters. Fissures spider outward, and with each fissure comes the sudden self-awareness that arises only out of an object as it breaks, which consists of astonishment and also disgust. And with disgust, a bacteria seeping up through the cracks, the period of decomposition begins.

~ ~ ~

5. *Anything irregular, bizarre, or otherwise departing from established rules and proportions. Odd, grotesque, exaggerated, and overdecorated.*

The inside of the outside is frosted like a cake. The gaze scarcely lands before it rolls and tumbles. There are ripples and curls and curves and hollows; peaks and troughs and eddies and crests. Nothing is still. Here and there, some frame or another makes a sensible effort, tries to pin down the corners of some particular escapade, but the inside of the outside spills out over the edges with abandon. Whole doorways disappear, consumed. The inside of the outside is foamy and thick and jumbles soundwaves. Its logic is bound up in gilt and crystal.

The inside of the inside, this breathing thing, swells and, meeting its edges, eddies and swirls.

~ ~ ~

History: Curling, then straight. Textured, then smooth. Hot, then cool. Loud, then quiet. Confection, then astringency. Elation, then sobriety. Passion, then reason. Indulgence, then abstinence. Tumult, then frame.

Then curling again. Then textured again. Then hot again. Then loud again. Then confection again. Then elation again. Then passion again. Then indulgence again. Then tumult again.

Then straight, then smooth, etc., etc.

~ ~ ~

6. *To instruct, to delight, to move. The divine was made physically present and palpable.*

Your bag is all wrong. It is new but cheap, and in every other way also wrong. It is too small. It is too brightly colored. The pattern is childish. Who are you anyway? You discard it after a single day, traumatized by your own poor choices, in exchange for a bag that is only mostly wrong, that you brought along in your suitcase for this very purpose, to hedge against this very likelihood.

How do they know, these ladies, so precisely how to be? The bags they carry are leather and quite voluminous—black, white, gray or camel. In these bags they stash objects pertaining to their beauty: little tools and magic pens and spells. Their bags are like portals into a Platonic ideal, the ideal of grace; thus, they are weightless. It is for them, these ladies, to diffuse this grace; it seeps from their bags, a contained quantity of the golden light in whose radiance Mary hovers. It channels through their little tools into perfect patterns across their skin. But how do they know how to use these tools? Trust, and a certain surrender of reason. It is as simple, perhaps, as not resisting, which means that you had a perfectly fine opportunity yourself. Just relax and your eyelids will bloom with color. What harm does it do? These ladies are not unhappy, and look how they enrich the world. Look how they shine upon all who pass.

~ ~ ~

7. *Religious themes with direct and emotional involvement. Horns of plenty, festoons, baby angels, the heads of lions holding rings in their mouths, female faces surrounded by garlands, oval cartouches, acanthus leaves, classical columns, caryatids, pediments. An overtly emotional and sensory appeal to the faithful.*

Acanthus leaves swarm the doorframes. The walls all but drip with love for themselves. Leaves and petals, scrolling foliage. What extravagance is this that spills so very far out beyond the bounds of necessity as to cover every single inch?—the walls, the ceiling, even the floor. A thousand tiny, tessellated tiles. Glorious peacocks in tessellated tiles.

This is wealth, one declares with disapproval and envy. And wealth, of course, contains within itself the elements of corruption. It contains within itself the suffering of the many. This scrolling foliage indicates the suffering of the many. It burgeons and blooms in marshes of privilege, where there is no wind, an affront to the actual persistence of poverty. Such is the calm in this enormous room that it floats like a kind of heaven on earth, high above the street with its sewage and noise, half tangled already in the clouds with the angels. That some are closer to heaven than others is a fact established by the room itself.

Today, we see that this is a lie. For one thing, this very same room is now filled with tourists. Tourists are the opposite of chosen; they choose themselves, charge in with their tickets, their maps and their cameras. They wander these rooms clutching their cameras muttering: How beautiful. How foolish. How delightful. How impractical. The tourists don't relate to the angels, who are left to mill about with no meaning. They know the rich are no closer to heaven than they are.

We absolve the corruption in a democratic spirit, assign care of these rooms to a nonprofit organization. Even the angels are no closer to heaven than we are. Meanwhile, wealth has removed itself to quieter quarters where it burgeons and blooms in other ways, in private apartments, on unknowable yachts. Wealth sails its yachts through the suffering of the many, through row boats piled with refugees, through schools of fish who are sweating and coughing up plastic, past pirates and government regulations. That some are more removed from government regulation than others is a fact established by the yacht itself.

~ ~ ~

8. *To create surprise and the illusion of motion.*

Powdered gypsum is mixed with water to form a stiff but workable paste. This paste is applied immediately upon hydration to the surface of a wall or possibly an armature and shaped as desired with metal tools. The hydrated plaster gradually hardens, expanding at first and then contracting slightly. It hardens into running scrolls, acanthus leaves, scrolling foliage, cherubim and the limbs and breasts of nameless women.

Plaster is suitable for finishing rather than load-bearing. It is susceptible to gilt; it absorbs and stabilizes liquid pigment. Unlike fabric, it can go on forever, drifting and curling across every wall.

Gypsum is a naturally forming non-metallic mineral whose structure consists of layers of calcium and sulfate ions bonded by sheets of anion water molecules. Its chemical formula is $CaSO_4 \cdot 2H_2O$. In its raw state, its luster is vitreous to silky, pearly, or waxy. Its diaphaneity is transparent to translucent. Its optical properties are biaxial. Some forms of gypsum are crystalline. In fact, the largest crystals ever found on earth have been gypsum crystals.

Imagine if all this gypsum crystalized at once and we stood as if in caves, walls sparkling with facets of pearly translucency, facet upon facet—bladed, columnar, cubic, dodecahedral, octahedral, prismatic, reticulated, sphenoid, tabular. The inside of the outside splinters and sprouts. Crystals gather and pile, almost tumble, look as if to tumble, hold, tumble more. Crystals cluster in the shapes of angels raising their hands to the heavens.

~ ~ ~

9. *Use of contrast, movement, exuberant detail, deep color, grandeur, and surprise to achieve a sense of awe.*

You buy a pair of expensive sandals. There is very little to them, just a few small patches of perfect leather. You love them intensely. For a time, you feel there is something to you. Or rather, there is something around the exterior of you against which the sound waves emitted by others can bounce and return with information pertaining to your shape and location.

You might ask, But don't I always wear shoes? I am not some hippie wandering dazed through the grass. But it is something else altogether to wear shoes that you love. Love fortifies where indifference does not. Or: It is something else altogether to wear expensive shoes. Expense fortifies where cheapness does not. Or: It is something else altogether to wear shoes that are truly well made. Or: It is something else altogether to wear shoes that are different from the shoes that other people wear. Or: It is something else altogether to wear shoes that are not available in department stores.

Is it because these sandals are expensive that you love them? They feel more solid to you than they actually are because you endow them with financial properties. Or is it because they are truly well made? You feel safer, you find, behind expensive and well-made things. It is a lesson that the ladies with the shoes and the bags have taught you. Now you want all of your things to be expensive and well made. It gives you a way to imagine existing in the world.

~ ~ ~

History: Humanity picked up a stick, examined it, turned it over a couple of times, and with a blade of grass tied it to another stick; it picked up a stone and stacked it on another stone. Cathedrals emerged, and castles with moats. Those in command of these resources declared themselves rich and encircled themselves in marble and satin, leaving the poor to make due with reeds and straw. Then the rich demanded billiard tables and humanity, naturally slow to acknowledge any impediment, was forced to admit there were only, in fact, so many elephants. That is, there were more rich demanding billiard balls than there were elephants to slaughter for the harvest of ivory, which would have been bad enough in itself but furthermore pointed to a much larger problem: that there is really, in this world, only so much of anything. Not only the rich but all of humanity raised their voices in protest against the limited world. Then a fellow with a gaze fixed firmly on the future began tinkering with nitrocellulose and camphor and developed the first synthetic polymer.

The plaster dried up, began to crack and chip, and across the walls spread plastic acanthus leaves and sheets of vinyl printed with enormous red letters and photographic images of women's skin. Humanity roared in triumph over the natural world, over the natural law of material scarcity, and the poor encircled themselves in drywall and rayon. Mary splintered into a thousand acrylic figurines and Venus dwindled down to two dimensions, a vision of bones and breasts draped in brand logos. Where humanity so much as waved its hand, synthetic polymers bloomed, lifeless and toxic but brightly colored. Now the dead walls are lined with magnets and keychains and humanity, gorged but yet increasingly malnourished, stumbles around groping after old things, things it still doesn't know how not to ruin and from which it must be cordoned off.

~ ~ ~

The monks in sandals stop you as you are crossing the piazza. What is it you covet, they demand, in those ladies shoes? You are embarrassed; you make efforts to moderate the word "covet." They say: Do not lay up for yourselves treasures on earth, where moth and rust destroy and where thieves break in and steal. You say: The shoes are the effect, not the cause. The monks begin to grow impatient.

They say: Look at us, all we sacrifice in the name of the sacred—look out our bare, dirty feet and homely faces. And you go around here wide eyed and gawking, falling for all their tricks. Yet you call yourself a woman of substance.

Yes, but they are at ease in a room full of mirrors, you say. They live with centuries behind them, in a beautiful language, and I am what? A kind of liquid that has no texture or weight, something like a passing coil of smoke. A woman of substance—what is substance anyway? Where exactly is it located, is it inside or outside? Is it form or content?

You've read books. You have thoughts. You possess certain skills, the monks in sandals say.

These buildings are made of stone and marble, you say, and they've been here for hundreds of years. Water and smoke course through them and still they remain. I course through them—I with my books and my thoughts am apparently nothing: they don't even quiver; they don't register even a single mark, even a single indentation. Their surfaces are lively and fertile and refute by means of their very existence all your peevish conceptions of substance. The ladies understand this. Is this not precisely what they're after, with their expensive shoes and their bags? To make of their bodies temples with marble walls?

A woman is more than a vessel waiting to be filled, the monks say.

The point is not the filling but the quality of the emptiness, you say. A temple is filled with beautiful silence.

The monks laugh at the comparison, knowing these ladies better than you do. They say, You mistake these buildings for something they're not. The fact that they're old doesn't make them eternal, or independent of human motivation and enterprise. The dragging cloak of history is not absolution.

But enduring as they have!, you assert in their defense.

These buildings are nothing but spasms of vanity. That they persist is a testament not to their virtue but merely their luck in escaping aerial bombing. What vanity builds, vanity is bound to one day destroy.

What do you know of architectural virtue?, you demand. And while we're on the topic of buildings and women, what it seems to me you elide in all your fist waving through the ages is this: What of beauty? What is it exactly and where does it live? Is it substance or form? What does it weigh?

Beauty is a yacht plowing through the suffering of the many.

But you, you monks, burned the many at the stake! You chopped the many into pieces, without remorse! You are not innocent. You did it all without the proffer of a single comfort.

Lay up for yourselves, the monks say, treasures in heaven, where neither moth nor rust destroys and where thieves do not break in and steal.

What is beauty if not the incarnation of heaven? Look up and the ceiling dissolves into a chorus of angels.

Paltry and inadequate! Meager and misguided! The monks grow animated, waving their arms. Oh how easily you are deceived! Men project their notions of heaven across all that they happen by way of their loins to covet: the walls of villas, the bodies of women. As a result, you suffer. You know your body is not in fact heaven but a marshy and unruly patch of earth, subject like every other patch of earth to natural cycles of decay. Yet rather than confront them with their apalling error, you convince yourself that you're in the wrong, that you're failing these men and possibly all of humanity by failing to create of yourself a hallowed container. You scramble instead to create some kind of illusion.

I speak not of my body but of Titian, Veronese, Tintoretto, Tiepolo. Men are fools, I agree, splashing reproductions of women's skin onto billboards. And if I suffer by that, it is my own stupidity. But Titian, Veronese, Tinteretto, Tiepolo—

You wish your body were Titian, Veronese, Tintoretto, Tiepolo. You want to dissolve yourself into curling plaster.

The monks have you here, and you are ashamed. Yes, you say, if it comes to that. What is this marshy patch of earth with all its latent treachery to art?

The monks' homely faces begin to soften. You were at best, they say, the blooming of a flower, and now you feel every day even less of even that. It's not a question of smoke but of soil you're trying to float up out of. You want some other kind of flower within yourself that will go on blooming in perpetuity and short of that, you want to float away. Poor child.

You are lulled for a moment by the monks' tender gaze, their capacity to see beyond themselves. But then you remember who you're dealing with here. You rouse yourself and declare with conviction: Burning the body at the stake is not the answer!

But to prove you wrong in some way you don't understand, the monks then ripple and slowly dissolve and there is no more arguing with them. They fill the piazza with the sound of a single cello, very faint and as if from a great distance. And what of language?, the cello asks. What of music? What of learning? What of love? What of sunlight?

~ ~ ~

10. *An obstacle in schematic logic. A large, irregularly-shaped pearl.*

When the sound waves emitted by others reach you, you wish them to return with a vision of grandeur and magnificence. You wish this so as to prove to yourself you are not nothing. But the inside is cluttered with mirrors at odd angles. The boundaries don't dissolve exactly but multiply; in fact, it's all a jumble in there. Is language form or content? Ornament or substance?

You give up. You go on. The inside, drawn in through this series of narrow canals, swells out again to span the breadth of an ocean, where there is no history, where there are no shapes, contained only by the shoreline of foreign continents.